SRA
Reading
Mastery®
Transformations

Language Arts
Textbook

Siegfried Engelmann

Bernadette Kelly

Karen Davis

Susie Andrist

Jerry Silbert

McGraw Hill

Acknowledgments

The authors are grateful to the following people for their assistance in the preparations of Reading Mastery Transformations Grade 2 Language.

Amilcar Cifuentes
Gary Davis
Cally Dwyer
Katherine Gries
Debbi Kleppen
Margie Mayo
Patricia McFadden
Melissa Morrow

Trevor Smith
Leta Tillitt
Piper VanNortwick
John Weber
Tina Wells
Nancy Woolfson
Mary Rosenbaum

PHOTO CREDITS

11 (t)Purestock/SuperStock, (c)McGraw-Hill Education, (b)Echo/Getty Images; 12 McGraw-Hill Education; 14 McGraw-Hill Education; 16 McGraw-Hill Education; 22 McGraw-Hill Education; 25 McGraw-Hill Education; 83 (l)Bryan Mullennix/age fotostock, (c)^UserGI15633745/iStock/Getty Images, (r)CrazyD/iStock/Getty Images; 88 Purestock/SuperStock; 104 (cw from top)Sebastian Schneider/Getty Images, (2)Robert Trevis-Smith/Getty Images, (3,4)George Bernard/Avalon Licensing Limited, (5)Justus de Cuveland/Getty Images; 105 Karen H. Black/Shutterstock; 106 (cw from top)Sebastian Schneider/Getty Images, (2)Robert Trevis-Smith/Getty Images, (3,4)George Bernard/Avalon Licensing Limited, (5)Justus de Cuveland/Getty Images; 108 John White Photos/Moment/Getty Images; 109 benmm/iStock/Getty Images; 110 David Cox/McGraw-Hill Education; 111 Ingram Publishing; 113 Michael Melford/Stockbyte/Getty Images; 118 tonda/iStock/Getty Images; 119 Ron Thomas/iStock/Getty Images; 121 (l)sozon/Shutterstock, (r)McGraw-Hill Education; 123 (tl)©Lusoimages-Sweets/Alamy Stock Photo, (tr)luxcreative/iStock/Getty Images, (bl)Joe DeGrandis/McGraw-Hill Education, (br)DougSchneiderPhoto/E+/Getty Images; 124 (t,cl)ivkuzmin/iStock/Getty Images, (cr)Ingram Publishing, (bl)amstockphoto/Shutterstock, (br)OJO Images Ltd./Alamy Stock Photo; 125 (tl,br)McGraw-Hill Education, (tr)racorn/123RF, (bl)Franco Nadalin/EyeEm/Getty Images; 126 (t)©BananaStock/Alamy Stock Photo, (bl)Dot Box Inc./McGraw-Hill Education, (bcl)McGraw-Hill Education, (bcr)Paul Bradbury/OJO Images/Getty Images, (br)imagenavi/Getty Images; 127 (tl)Hero Images/Getty Images, (tr)©Andrew Olney/age fotostock, (bl)McGraw-Hill Education, (br)©David Schaffer/age fotostock; 128 (tl,bl)McGraw-Hill Education, (tr)Franco Nadalin/EyeEm/Getty Images, (br)racorn/123RF.

mheducation.com/prek-12

Send all inquiries to:
McGraw-Hill Education
8787 Orion Place
Columbus, OH 43240

ISBN: 978-0-07-905415-9
MHID: 0-07-905415-3

Printed in the United States of America.

2 3 4 5 6 7 8 9 10 LWI 26 25 24 23 22 21

A **Write reports if the sentence reports what the picture shows. Write no if the sentence does not report.**

1. The children had been camping for three days.

2. A girl gave something to a dog.

3. The girls liked chicken.

4. Two girls and a boy sat at a picnic table.

5. Cups and plates were on the table.

6. The boy petted the dog.

7. The boy wanted to go home.

A.	
1.	
2.	
3.	
4.	
5.	
6.	
7.	

END OF LESSON 4

A **Write reports if the sentence reports what the picture shows.
Write no if the sentence does not report.**

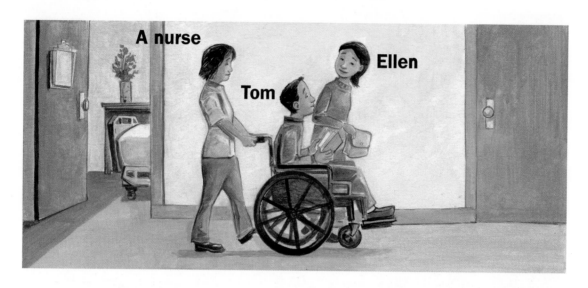

Rule: Sentences that report tell what the picture shows.

1. Tom sat in a wheelchair.

2. Tom's sister walked next to him.

3. A nurse pushed a wheelchair.

4. The nurse felt very warm.

5. Tom was hungry.

6. Tom wore slippers and a hat.

A.	
1.	
2.	
3.	
4.	
5.	
6.	

END OF LESSON 5

A **Write reports if the sentence reports what the picture shows. Write no if the sentence does not report.**

1. The woman rode a horse.

2. The horse was named Rusty.

3. The woman wore a dress and sunglasses.

4. The woman lived on a farm.

5. A man sat on a fence.

6. The man held a rope.

7. The man wanted to ride the horse.

END OF LESSON 6

A **Write reports if the sentence reports what the picture shows. Write no if the sentence does not report.**

1. Mr. Jones stood in front of his desk.

2. Mr. Jones wore a shirt and tie.

3. Devon wrote on the whiteboard.

4. Devon was a very good speller.

5. One girl raised her hand.

6. Hilary held a piece of paper.

7. The room had desks in it.

8. Hilary raised her hand.

B **Write sentences that report on the picture.**

1.	▮▮▮▮▮▮▮▮▮▮	held an umbrella.
2.	▮▮▮▮▮▮▮▮▮▮	chased a cat.
3.	▮▮▮▮▮▮▮▮▮▮	fell on the sidewalk.

END OF LESSON 7

A Write **reports** if the sentence reports what the picture shows. Write **no** if the sentence does not report.

1. Bill and Carlos sat in chairs.

2. Nancy read a book about horses.

3. The dogs dreamed about a bone.

4. Boots were on a shelf.

5. All the firefighters played cards.

6. Everybody wanted to go home.

7. Two dogs were lying on the floor.

B **Write sentences that report on the picture.**

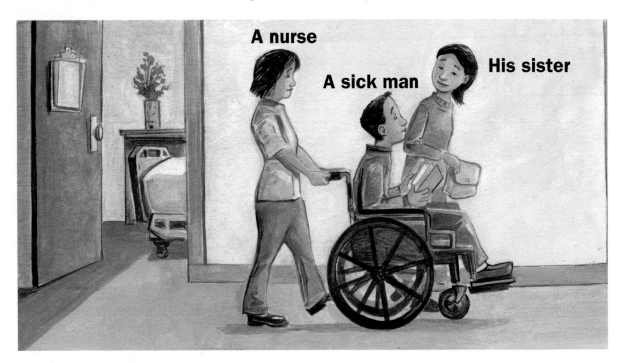

A nurse

A sick man

His sister

1.	▬▬▬▬▬▬	pushed the wheelchair.
2.	▬▬▬▬▬▬	sat in the wheelchair.
3.	▬▬▬▬▬▬	walked next to the man.

A Copy the sentence that tells the main thing the person did.

1.

Kayla

Kayla held a glass.

Kayla drank a glass of water.

Kayla wore a belt.

2.

Jill

Jill bent her leg.

Jill held the board with one hand.

Jill sawed a board.

END OF LESSON q

A Copy the sentence that tells the main thing the person did.

1. Chen

2. Martha

Chen stood next to the tub.

Chen gave the dog a bath.

Chen held a brush in one hand.

Martha wore overalls.

Martha reached over her head.

Martha painted part of the house.

B Copy each sentence just as it is written.

1.	How did he do that?	
2.	The girl had 3 red hats.	
3.	Eli and Rosa worked hard today.	

C Write <u>reports</u> if the sentence reports what the picture shows. Write <u>no</u> if the sentence does not report.

1. Maria is pushing a red bike.

2. Maria got her bike for her birthday.

3. Linda jumps rope every day.

4. Jim is pushing his brother's bike.

5. A car is parked on the street.

6. Linda is jumping rope.

7. The children are best friends.

END OF LESSON 10

A **Copy the sentence that tells the main thing the person did.**

1.

Kevin sat in a canoe.

Kevin loved the water.

Kevin paddled a canoe.

2.

A woman held a broom.

A woman swept the floor.

A woman wore a dress.

3.

Pam shoveled snow.

Pam stood in the snow.

Pam had a shovel.

END OF LESSON 11

A Write the letter of each picture that shows what the sentence says.

A.

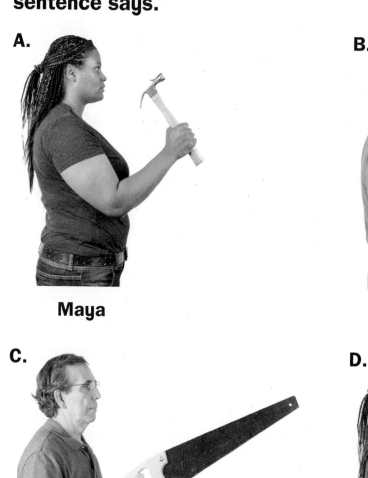

Maya

B.

Seth

C.

Seth

D.

Maya

1. A person held a hammer.

2. Seth held a tool.

3. Seth held a hammer.

4. A person held a tool.

END OF LESSON 13

A **Write a sentence that reports on the main thing each person did.**

1.

Beth

2.

Rosa

| painted | book | ceiling | read |

Check CP: Does each sentence begin with a capital letter and end with a period?

Check M: Does each sentence tell the main thing the person did?

Check SP: Did you spell the words from the word list correctly?

B **Write the letter of each picture that shows what the sentence says.**

A.

Marcos

B.

Ashley

C.

Marcos

D.

Ashley

1. Marcos held a container.

2. Ashley held a jar.

3. A person held a container.

4. Ashley held a container.

A **Write a sentence that reports on the main thing each person did.**

1. **A zookeeper**

2. **Bob**

3. **Mr. Briggs**

banana	pizza	cheese	campfire	lit
built	gave	put	made	

Check CP: Does each sentence begin with a capital letter and end with a period?

Check M: Does each sentence tell the main thing the person did?

Check SP: Did you spell the words from the word list correctly?

Write the letter of each picture that shows what the sentence says.

A.

Eli

B.

Anna

C.

Anna

D.

Eli

1. Eli ate fruit.

2. A person ate fruit.

3. Anna ate an apple.

4. A person ate a banana.

END OF LESSON 15

A Write a sentence that reports on the main thing each person did.

1.

Vic

2.

A woman

watering can	watered	ax	
plant	tree	hanging	chopped

Check CP: Does each sentence begin with a capital letter and end with a period?

Check M: Does each sentence tell the main thing the person did?

Check SP: Did you spell the words from the word list correctly?

Write the letter of each picture that shows what the sentence says.

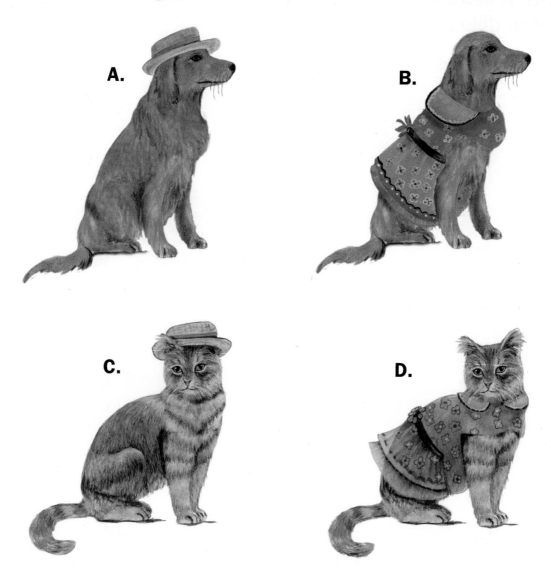

A.

B.

C.

D.

1. An animal wore clothing.

2. An animal wore a dress.

3. A dog wore clothing.

4. A cat wore a hat.

END OF LESSON 16

A **Write a sentence that reports on the main thing that happened.**

1. **Fred and Bill**

2. **A small dog**

3. **A girl**

| soccer | hoop | watched | through | TV |

Check CP: Does each sentence begin with a capital letter and end with a period?

Check M: Does each sentence tell the main thing that happened?

Check SP: Did you spell the words from the word list correctly?

END OF LESSON 17

A **Write a sentence that reports on the main thing each person did.**

1.
Ramon

2.
Yoshi

3.
Jerry and Ann

poured	toasted	put
carried	soup	campfire	marshmallows

Check CP: Does each sentence begin with a capital letter and end with a period?

Check M: Does each sentence tell the main thing the person did?

Check SP: Did you spell the words from the word list correctly?

END OF LESSON 18

A **Write a sentence that reports on the main thing that happened.**

That magician

1.

Hiro and his sister

2.

The carpenter

3.

jumped	carried	pulled
fence	boards	rabbit	over

Check CP: Does each sentence begin with a capital letter and end with a period?

Check M: Does each sentence tell the main thing the person did?

Check SP: Did you spell the words from the word list correctly?

Write the letter of each picture that shows what the sentence says.

A.

Maya

B.

Seth

C.

Seth

D.

Maya

1. He held a tool.

2. She held a hammer.

3. A person held a tool.

4. She held a tool.

C Copy the paragraph.

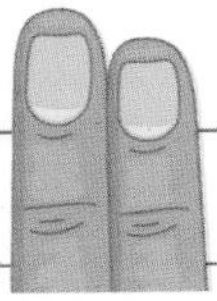

A bird fell out of a tree. It

landed on the ground. A boy picked

it up. He took it home.

Check I: Did you indent the first line?

Check CP: Does each sentence begin with a capital letter and end with a period?

Check SP: Did you spell each word correctly?

END OF LESSON 19

A Write a sentence that reports on the main thing that happened.

1.

A dog and a clown

2.

The airplane

| flew | walked | tightrope | bridge | across | under |

Check CP: Does each sentence begin with a capital letter and end with a period?

Check M: Does each sentence tell the main thing that happened?

Check SP: Did you spell the words from the word list correctly?

	Ellen helped her dad fix the car.
	She worked on the brakes. Ellen and
	her dad fixed the car in three hours.

Check I: Did you indent the first line?

Check CP: Does each sentence begin with a capital letter and end with a period?

Check SP: Did you spell each word correctly?

C **Work each item.**

> • He pushed a vehicle.
>
> • She pushed a vehicle.
>
> • A person pushed a vehicle.

1. Copy the sentence that tells about **all** the pictures.

2. Copy the sentence that tells about **only one** picture.

3. Copy the sentence that tells about **two** pictures.

END OF LESSON 20

A **Write a sentence that reports on the main thing each person did.**

1.

The boy

2.

A girl

| teeth | brushed | kicked | toothbrush | football |

Check CP: Does each sentence begin with a capital letter and end with a period?

Check M: Does each sentence tell the main thing the person did?

Check SP: Did you spell the words from the word list correctly?

B Copy the paragraph.

	Jason had a bad day. He missed
	breakfast because he woke up late.
	He had to walk to school in the rain.

Check I: Did you indent the first line?

Check CP: Does each sentence begin with a capital letter and end with a period?

Check SP: Did you spell each word correctly?

C Work each item.

- A person sat on an animal.
- He sat on an animal.
- Melissa sat on an animal.

 Tom  Melissa  Melissa

1. Copy the sentence that tells about **two** pictures.
2. Copy the sentence that tells about **all** the pictures.
3. Copy the sentence that tells about **only one** picture.

END OF LESSON 21

A **Write a sentence that reports on the main thing each person did.**

1.

That old man

2.

A tall boy

branch   water   sawed

Check CP: Does each sentence begin with a capital letter and end with a period?

Check M: Does each sentence tell the main thing the person did?

Check SP: Did you spell the words from the word list correctly?

B **Copy the paragraph.**

	An eagle sat in a tree. It looked up
	into the sky. A big jet flew by. The eagle
	started to cry.

Check I: Did you indent the first line?

Check CP: Does each sentence begin with a capital letter and end with a period?

Check SP: Did you spell each word correctly?

C **Work each item.**

- An animal sat on a bike.
- A dog sat on a vehicle.
- An animal sat on a vehicle.

1. Copy the sentence that tells about **only one** picture.
2. Copy the sentence that tells about **all** the pictures.
3. Copy the sentence that tells about **two** pictures.

END OF LESSON 22

A **Write a sentence that reports on the main thing each animal did.**

1.

A bear

2.

A monkey

| walked | juggled | three | tightrope | across |

Check CP: Does each sentence begin with a capital letter and end with a period?

Check M: Does each sentence tell the main thing the animal did?

Check SP: Did you spell the words from the word list correctly?

END OF LESSON 23

A **Write a sentence that reports on the main thing each group did.**

1.

2.

| cleaned | elephant | basketball | washed |

Check CP: Does each sentence begin with a capital letter and end with a period?

Check M: Does each sentence tell the main thing the group did?

Check SP: Did you spell the words from the word list correctly?

Write two sentences that report on the person.

- First tell the main thing the person did.
- Then tell something else about the person.

Mr. Harmon

radio   mopped   listened   floor   kitchen   boots

A **Write a sentence that reports on the main thing each group did.**

1.

2.

| stream | room | cleaned | crossed |

Check CP: Does each sentence begin with a capital letter and end with a period?

Check M: Does each sentence tell the main thing the group did?

Check SP: Did you spell the words from the word list correctly?

B **Write two sentences that report on the person.**

- First tell the main thing the person did.
- Then tell something else about the person.

1. A girl

2. Arthur

baseball   caught   stood   glove   muscles
chopped   ax   uniform   fence

A THE CASE OF THE MISSING CORN

1.

2.

A COMPOUND WORDS

1. waterfall

2. sailboat

3. bookshelf

4. fireside

INDEPENDENT WORK

B Copy each sentence. Then circle the subject.

1. Five cats were on the roof.

2. They read two funny books.

3. A red bird landed on the roof.

4. A dog and a cat played in their yard.

5. It stopped.

END OF LESSON 27

A COMPOUND WORDS

1. lighthouse

2. shoebox

3. toothbrush

4. fireball

5. lamppost

INDEPENDENT WORK

B Copy the paragraph. Circle each subject. Then draw a picture.

	Sara and Rod painted the kitchen
	blue. Sara had a paintbrush. Rod used
	a roller. They stopped to eat lunch. She
	laughed. The windows were blue!

END OF LESSON 28

A WORDS THAT ARE CAPITALIZED

- A person's name is always capitalized.
- Days of the week are always capitalized.
- Months of the year are always capitalized.

1. January
2. Sunday
3. Tuesday
4. September
5. James

B For each item, write day, month, or name.

1. Jay Turner
2. October
3. Wednesday
4. Friday
5. Mr. Briggs
6. David
7. December

C Rewrite each item so that it has a word with an apostrophe.

1. the dress that belongs to the girl
2. the tent that belongs to Bob
3. the toys that belong to my cat
4. the watch that belongs to that boy
5. a hammer that belongs to his mother
6. the legs that belong to my father

END OF LESSON 29

A For each item, write <u>day</u>, <u>month</u>, or <u>name</u>.

1. Fran

2. November

3. Saturday

4. Mrs. Brown

5. July

6. Norman Nelson

7. Monday

INDEPENDENT WORK

B Write a sentence that tells the main thing each group did.

1.

2.

| trick | circus | supper |

END OF LESSON 30

A **Write a sentence that tells about <u>all</u> the pictures. Then write a sentence for each picture.**

1.　　　　　　　　2.　　　　　　　　3.

| the seat of | small | the back of | big | the arm of |

	████████████████████████ .	
1.	A ████████ dog sat on ████████ a chair.	
2.	A ████████ dog sat on ████████ a chair.	
3.	A ████████ dog sat on ████████ a chair.	

A **Write a sentence that tells about <u>all</u> the pictures. Then write a sentence for each picture.**

1.   2.   3.

| knee | blue | arm | head | yellow |

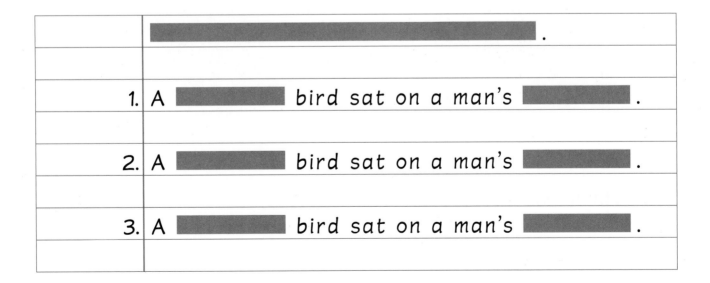

	▮▮▮▮▮▮▮▮▮▮▮▮▮▮ .
1.	A ▮▮▮▮▮ bird sat on a man's ▮▮▮▮▮ .
2.	A ▮▮▮▮▮ bird sat on a man's ▮▮▮▮▮ .
3.	A ▮▮▮▮▮ bird sat on a man's ▮▮▮▮▮ .

END OF LESSON 32

A **Write a sentence about both pictures. Then write a sentence that tells only about picture B.**

B.

C.

1. The window has   .
2. The window has   .

B.

C.

3. The house has   .
4. The house has   .

END OF LESSON 33

A **Write a sentence about both pictures. Then write a sentence that tells only about picture B.**

B.   **C.**

1. The boy wore ▬▬▬▬▬▬ .
2. The boy wore ▬▬▬▬▬▬▬ .

A Write a good sentence for each group.

1.

2.

| opened | presents | water | pool | their |

Check CP: Does each sentence begin with a capital letter and end with a period?

Check M: Does each sentence tell the main thing the group did?

Check SP: Did you spell the words from the word list correctly?

END OF LESSON 36

A **Write a paragraph. Begin with a good sentence about the women. Then write a sentence about each person. Tell the main thing each person did.**

hammer   side   board   nail   saw   paint

Check CP: Does each sentence begin with a capital letter and end with a period?

Check M: Does each sentence tell the main thing?

Check SP: Did you spell the words from the word list correctly?

END OF LESSON 37

A **Write a paragraph. First tell the main thing the group did. Then tell the main thing each person did.**

| washed | floor | picked | swept | dirt |
| toys | rug | pile | scrubbed | under |

Check CP: Does each sentence begin with a capital letter and end with a period?

Check M: Does each sentence tell the main thing?

Check SP: Did you spell the words from the word list correctly?

END OF LESSON 38

A **Write a paragraph. First tell the main thing the group did. Then tell the main thing each person did.**

fried	poured	potato	soup
pieces	hamburgers	outdoors	sliced	fire

Check CP: Does each sentence begin with a capital letter and end with a period?

Check M: Does each sentence tell the main thing?

Check SP: Did you spell the words from the word list correctly?

A **Write a paragraph. First tell the main thing the group did. Then tell the main thing each animal did.**

A bear

A seal   A poodle

| bicycle | balanced | through | nose | its | ball |

Check CP: Does each sentence begin with a capital letter and end with a period?

Check M: Does each sentence tell the main thing?

Check SP: Did you spell the words from the word list correctly?

END OF LESSON 40

A **Write a paragraph. First tell the main thing the group did. Then tell the main thing each person did.**

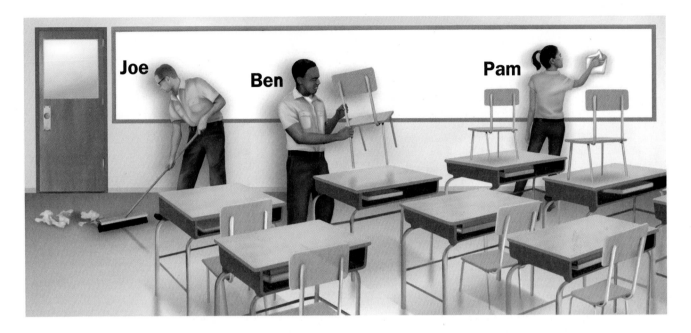

| board | desk | chair | cleaned | classroom | janitors |

Check CP: Does each sentence begin with a capital letter and end with a period?

Check M: Does each sentence tell the main thing?

Check SP: Did you spell the words from the word list correctly?

END OF LESSON 41

A Write a paragraph. First tell the main thing the group did. Then tell the main thing each person did.

Raymond   Sally   Jill

| gardeners | yard | carried | saw | plant |
| shovel | work | branch | hole |

Check CP: Does each sentence begin with a capital letter and end with a period?

Check M: Does each sentence tell the main thing?

Check SP: Did you spell the words from the word list correctly?

END OF LESSON 42

A **Write a clear paragraph.**

| snake | striped | large | wooden | cowgirl |

wearing   boots   outfit   young   basket

_____ fell out of a large old tree. It landed on the soft ground. _____ picked it up. _____ put it in a _____ and took it home.

Check CP: Does each sentence begin with a capital letter and end with a period?

Check Clear: Does each sentence give a clear picture of what happened?

Check SP: Did you spell the words from the word list correctly?

END OF LESSON 43

A **Write a clear paragraph.**

beard	sailor suits	parrot	monkeys
	shoulder	three	bald

_____ sat on _____ . _____ sat on _____ . He held _____ in one hand. He tossed _____ with the other hand. Three _____ picked up the _____ .

Check CP: Does each sentence begin with a capital letter and end with a period?

Check Clear: Does each sentence give a clear picture of what happened?

Check SP: Did you spell the words from the word list correctly?

END OF LESSON 44

A Rewrite the paragraph so each sentence gives a clear picture.

skunks

muscles

tattoo

pie

piece

_____ was carrying _____ . He saw _____ . He dropped _____ and climbed up _____ . _____ ate _____ . _____ looked up at the man.

Check CP: Does each sentence begin with a capital letter and end with a period?

Check Clear: Does each sentence give a clear picture of what happened?

Check SP: Did you spell the words from the word list correctly?

END OF LESSON 46

A Write a paragraph that reports on what happened. Write a sentence for each name shown in the pictures.

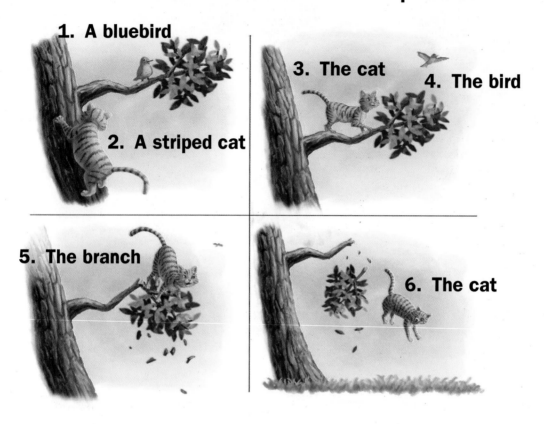

1. A bluebird
2. A striped cat
3. The cat
4. The bird
5. The branch
6. The cat

ground	climbed	flew	jumped
broke	trunk	branch	

Check M: Does each sentence tell the main thing?

Check CP: Does each sentence begin with a capital letter and end with a period?

Check DID: Does each sentence tell what something did?

END OF LESSON 49

A

| baseball | river | black | towel | happy |
| young | wide | brown | large |

INDEPENDENT WORK

B Write the contraction for each word pair.

1. had not

2. they would

3. you will

4. we are

5. here is

6. should not

END OF LESSON 50

A Write a paragraph that reports on what happened. Write a sentence for each name shown in the pictures.

| fell | ground | charged | toward | barrel |
| knocked | air | helped | away | walk |

Check M: Does each sentence tell the main thing?

Check CP: Does each sentence begin with a capital letter and end with a period?

Check DID: Does each sentence tell what somebody or something did?

END OF LESSON 51

A Write a paragraph that reports on what happened. Write a sentence for each name shown in the pictures.

1. Emily
3. The ball
2. Robert

5. Rover
4. It

6. The skunk

7. Robert and Emily

missed	Robert's head	threw	held	smelled
their	too high	toward	stink	chased

Check M: Does each sentence tell the main thing?

Check CP: Does each sentence begin with a capital letter and end with a period?

Check DID: Does each sentence tell what somebody or something did?

END OF LESSON 53

A Write a paragraph that reports on what happened. Write a sentence for each name shown in the pictures.

3. His sister

2. James

1. A little bird

4. James

5. She

bird	helped	fell	its nest
ground	climbed	tree	branch

Check M: Does each sentence tell the main thing?

Check CP: Does each sentence begin with a capital letter and end with a period?

Check DID: Does each sentence tell what somebody or something did?

END OF LESSON 55

A **Write a paragraph that reports on what happened. Write a sentence for each name shown in the pictures.**

1. Hector
2. He
3. A monkey
4. The monkey
5. Hector

grabbed	windowsill	started	yelled
ate	piece	pie	answer	phone	scolded

Check M: Tell the main thing.

Check CP: Begin with a capital letter and end with a period.

Check DID: Tell what somebody or something did.

END OF LESSON 57

A **Write a paragraph that reports on what happened. Write a sentence for each number shown in the pictures.**

barrel	rolled	truck	crashed
an apple	teacher	boy	caught

Check EH: Tell everything that happened.

Check CP: Begin with a capital letter and end with a period.

Check DID: Tell what somebody or something did.

A Write the name of each thing in the word list that is different in picture 1 and picture 2.

the glass   bowl of fruit   boy   pajamas
cat   milk in the glass   wall

END OF LESSON 60

A **Write a paragraph that reports on what happened.**

gorilla	walked	bananas	trail	cage
picked	escaped	followed	zookeeper	

Check EH: Tell everything that happened.

Check SP: Spell words from the word list correctly.

Check CP: Begin with a capital letter and end with a period.

Check DID: Tell what somebody or something did.

Write the name of each thing in the list that is different in picture 1 and picture 2.

| the horse | boy | boy's hat | cowboy |
| the cowboy's hat | | mountain | |

END OF LESSON 61

A Write a paragraph for the missing picture. Tell about the candle, the newspapers, and the woman.

1.

2.

3.

bucket   fell   burn   picked up

END OF LESSON 62

A **Write a paragraph that reports on what happened.**

flying disc   threw   field   Alex   bushes

bear   cub   mother   appeared   grabbed

Check EH: Tell everything that happened.

Check SP: Spell words from the word list correctly.

Check CP: Begin with a capital letter and end with a period.

Check DID: Tell what somebody or something did.

B **Tell what happened in the missing picture. Tell about Bill, the horse, and Lisa.**

1.

Lisa

Bill

The horse

2.

3.

A Write a paragraph for the missing picture. Tell about the baker, the flyswatter, and the pie.

2.

3.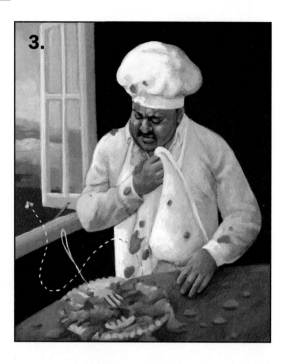

| pie | flyswatter | swung | splattered |

INDEPENDENT WORK

B Copy each word. Then write the correct meaning.

1. disagree   • the opposite of agree   • agree again

2. resend   • the opposite of send   • send again

3. remake   • the opposite of make   • make again

4. unwrap   • the opposite of wrap   • wrap again

END OF LESSON 64

A   RELATED WORDS

> land

1. land<u>slide</u>
2. land<u>ing</u>
3. <u>home</u>land

B   Write a paragraph for the missing picture.

1.

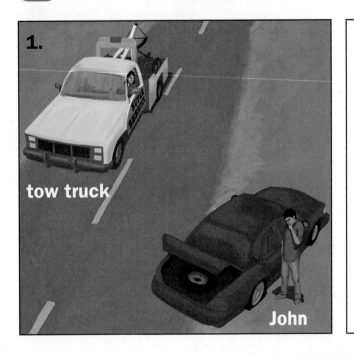

tow truck

John

2.

3.

SUPER SERVICE

---

tow truck   helped   jack

lifted   spare tire   parked   wheel

Check EH: Tell everything that happened in the middle picture.

Check Sentences: Write all your sentences correctly (**SP, CP, DID**).

A Write a paragraph for the missing picture.

1. mother bear

net

butterfly

Mr. Wingate

2.

3.

| climbed | growled | against | bush |
| missed | bear's head | swung | |

Check EH: Tell everything that happened in the middle picture.

Check Sentences: Write all your sentences correctly (**SP, CP, DID**).

B HOW THINGS FEEL

1. soft   2. hard   3. crunchy   4. chewy   5. juicy

END OF LESSON 67

A Write a paragraph for the missing picture.

2.

| banana | climbed | basket | flew | untangled | leash |

Check EH: Tell everything that happened in the middle picture.

Check Sentences: Write all your sentences correctly (**SP, CP, DID**).

A **Tell what happened in the first picture and the missing picture.**

1.

Carlos

Henry

2.

3.

Mr. Lopez

alarm clock	boots	poles	o'clock	outside	drove

	Carlos and Henry decided to go fishing
	on Saturday.

Check EH-1: Tell everything that happened in the first picture.

Check EH-2: Tell everything that happened in the middle picture.

Check S: Write all your sentences correctly (**SP, CP, DID**).

END OF LESSON 71

A Tell what happened in the first picture and the missing picture.

2.

| horse | followed | tied | skates | walked | through |

	Sandra decided to take her dog ice
	skating at the pond.

Check EH-1: Tell everything that happened in the first picture.

Check EH-2: Tell everything that happened in the middle picture.

Check S: Write all your sentences correctly (**SP, CP, DID**).

END OF LESSON 73

A **Tell what happened in the first picture and the missing picture.**

2.

3.

| ice | barricade | icy water | frozen | skate | walked | board |

	Sally went skating on a frozen pond. She
	took her dog Alex with her.

Check EH-1: Tell everything that happened in the first picture.

Check EH-2: Tell everything that happened in the middle picture.

Check S: Write all your sentences correctly (**SP, CP, DID**).

END OF LESSON 75

A **Write a paragraph that tells what happened in the first picture and the missing picture.**

1.

Fred

2.

3.

| knock | paint | shoes | lawn | hose | wash |

		Fred was painting a chair black. He was
		on his back porch.

Check EH-1: Tell everything that happened in the first picture.

Check EH-2: Tell everything that happened in the middle picture.

Check S: Write all your sentences correctly (**SP, CP, DID**).

END OF LESSON 77

A **Write a paragraph about Ann and Dan.**

 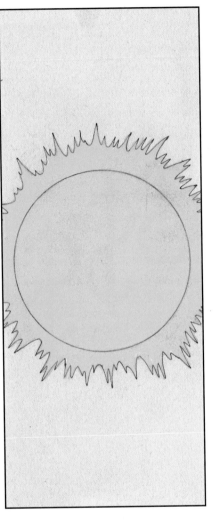 

movie   should   bike   helmet   decided   country   enjoyed

	Ann and Dan were thinking of what to do
	on Saturday. Ann thought .
	Dan thought .

END OF LESSON 79

A Write a paragraph about Sid and his dad.

motor	mower	lawn	should
push	money	cost	unhappy

	Their old lawn mower could not be fixed.
	Sid thought ▨▨▨▨▨. His dad thought
	▨▨▨▨.

A **Figure out which picture Zelda drew.**

Donna and her mother watched the tiny spiders. They were upside down in their web.

B **Write all the words that tell <u>when</u> or <u>how</u>.**

sat ▆▆▆▆▆▆▆

chair   still   wall   happy   alone   quietly   silly

INDEPENDENT WORK

C **Write the correct name for each item.**

1. a group of cows

2. a group of ships

3. a group of fish

4. a group of lions

END OF LESSON 82

A Write a description for each picture. Tell where the girls were and what they were doing.

1.

2.

B

1. yellow   2. good   3. often   4. freely

5. slowly   6. big   7. gently

END OF LESSON 83

A Write a description for each picture. Tell where the women were and what they were doing.

1.

2.

A **Write a description for the picture. Tell where the boys were and what they were doing.**

living room   lying   watching   sitting

END OF LESSON 85

A Write a description for each picture.

1. Mrs. Hart

her dog

2.

3.

4.

| tripped | watched | edge | grabbed | coat | cliff |

Check WAS: Does the first part of your story tell what Mrs. Hart **was doing** and what her dog **was doing?**

Check DID: Do the rest of your sentences tell what Mrs. Hart **did** and what her dog **did?**

END OF LESSON 86

A **Write a paragraph.**

Terry digs a hole in a field.

This is what he finds as he digs.

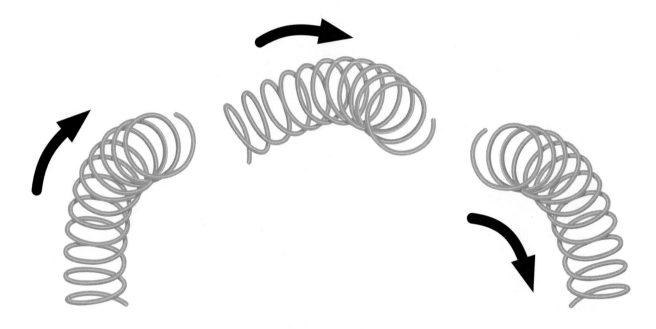

	A spring is . I know my
	answer is right because .
	Also, .

END OF LESSON 88

A Write a paragraph.

  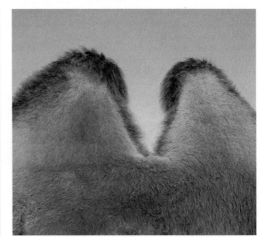

	These parts belong to a ▆▆▆▆ . I know
	my answer is right because ▆▆▆▆▆ .
	Also, ▆▆▆▆ .

INDEPENDENT WORK

B Put these words in alphabetical order. Word 1 is <u>rolled</u>.

1. ▆▆▆
2. ▆▆▆
3. ▆▆▆
4. ▆▆▆
5. ▆▆▆
6. ▆▆▆
7. ▆▆▆

team
stone
rolled
vent
well
unpack
x-ray

END OF LESSON 89

A Write a passage about trees.

roots	branches	spring
trunk	leaves	summer
bark	winter	fall

Trees

I have learned a lot ______. I learned that ______. I learned that ______. I learned that ______.

I think that trees ______. The thing I like most is ______.

B GUIDE WORDS

1. fox   kite

2. mask   queen

3. boy   friend

4. race   window

END OF LESSON 90

A Write a passage about insects.

temperature	beetle	butterfly	grasshopper
bee	cold blooded	body	water strider

	Insects
	I have learned ▓▓▓▓▓▓. I have seen
	▓▓▓▓▓▓. I learned ▓▓▓▓▓▓. I
	learned ▓▓▓▓▓▓. I learned ▓▓▓▓▓▓.
	I think that insects ▓▓▓▓▓▓. My
	favorite insect is ▓▓▓▓▓▓.

B GUIDE WORDS

1. | goal | love |

2. | van | zoo |

3. | holding | master |

END OF LESSON 91

A Write the letters that words on each page could begin with.

1. able   foolish

2. oat   summer

3. race   window

B Write a story that tells what the pictures show.

then   suddenly   stroller   finally   soon

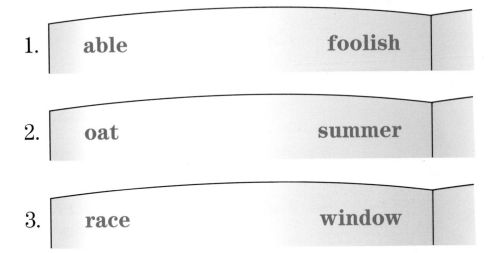

Misty   Aiden

4.

END OF LESSON 92

A Write a friend and tell about your new pet puppy. Your puppy is black and white and very small.

(Date)

(Greeting)

(Closing)

B Write a passage about water.

salty	temperature	living things	ocean

	Water
	I have learned ⬛⬛⬛. I have learned
	⬛⬛. I have learned ⬛⬛.
	I have learned ⬛⬛. I like to
	⬛⬛. I also like to ⬛⬛.

END OF LESSON 93

A Write a story about the picture.

Mr. Briggs Forgot Something

cash register   embarrassed   money   wallet
suddenly   blushed   angry   Rosy's Cafe

A

beach	rooster	gold coins	bushes	trees
ten	sand	turkeys	money	

B **WHAT'S YOUR OPINION?**

Opinion	1. Sell the white horse
	2. Sell five brown horses
	3. Raise the money some other way

END OF LESSON 95

A Write your opinion about what Greg should do.

Greg has saved over $300. He wants to buy a new bike that has racing handlebars, but the bike he has is in good shape. The new bike costs $350, but he could get at least $100 for the bike he has. In your opinion, what should Greg do?

In my opinion, Greg should ____________ . I think he should do that because ____________ .

B Write a story about the picture.

A Dream Vacation

- Tell where they worked and what their job was.
- Tell what they wanted to do.
- Tell why they were not doing those things.

factory	beach	island	at last	enjoyed
horseback	later	wonderful	decided	

END OF LESSON 96

A Write your opinion about what Maria should do.

> Maria is 16 years old. She wants to quit school. Her parents think quitting is a mistake. Maria is good at art, and she thinks she can sell the pictures she paints. Her dad's opinion is that she should stay in school and paint pictures during the summer. Then she could see if anybody would buy them.

In my opinion, Maria should ▮▮▮▮▮▮▮▮▮. I think she should do that because ▮▮▮▮▮▮▮▮.

B

A **Write your opinion about what the class should do.**

In our opinion, the class should ▭ . We think the class should do that because ▭ .

B **Write a story about the picture.**

A Night to Remember

spaceship	creature	grabbed	suddenly
frightened	trapped	finally	

A **Write your opinion about what Nina's family should do.**

Nina wants a puppy, but her family rents their apartment. Renters can't have dogs. They can have smaller pets. Her mother likes cats, but she doesn't want to be the one who feeds it or takes care of it. Nina's father does not like cats much, but he wouldn't mind a cat if somebody else took care of it. He likes fish, but he wouldn't feed them or keep the fish tank clean.

Nina's family had a problem. (Tell about the problem.) In my opinion, the family should ▬▬▬▬▬▬▬ . I think this is a good idea because ▬▬▬▬▬▬ . Also, ▬▬▬▬▬▬ . That's why I think it's better to ▬▬▬▬▬▬ .

INDEPENDENT WORK

B **Write all the letters that words on each page can begin with.**

1. car   goat

2. kettle   money

3. open   rainbow

END OF LESSON 100

A Write your opinion about what Ted should do.

Ted found a wallet in front of a toy store. It had $60 in it. Ted wanted to take some of the money, but he knew that would be stealing. In your opinion, what should he do?

Ted had a problem. (Tell about the problem.) In my opinion,
Ted should ▮▮▮▮▮▮▮▮▮▮ . I think this is a good idea because
▮▮▮▮▮▮▮▮▮ . Also, ▮▮▮▮▮▮▮▮▮ . I think that is why Ted
should ▮▮▮▮▮▮▮ .

B ALPHABETICAL ORDER

a b c d e f g h i j k l m
n o p q r s t u v w x y z

1. every

2. great

3. horse

4. kite

5. open

6. wing

C Write the words in alphabetical order.

stool

game

poke

into

dig

lamp

END OF LESSON 101

A **Write your opinion about what Ms. Evans should do.**

> Ms. Evans has a bad cold. She has an important meeting to go to, but she doesn't want to make anybody else sick. In your opinion, what should she do?

Ms. Evans has a problem. (Tell about the problem.) In my opinion, Ms. Evans should ▰▰▰▰▰▰▰ . I think this is a good idea because ▰▰▰▰▰ . Also, ▰▰▰▰▰ . That's why I think Ms. Evans should ▰▰▰▰▰ .

B **Write the words in alphabetical order.**

a b c d e f g h i j k l m n o p q r s t u v w x y z

1. ▰▰▰▰▰
2. ▰▰▰▰▰
3. ▰▰▰▰▰
4. ▰▰▰▰▰
5. ▰▰▰▰▰
6. ▰▰▰▰▰

homework

carrot

million

elephant

north

jail

END OF LESSON 102

A **Write a report.**

Something I Am Proud Of

I did something I am proud of (tell when). I was (tell where). I was there because (tell why). (Tell what happened. Tell what you did that you are proud of. Tell about all the important things.)

B **Write the letters in the order things happened in the story.**

A

B

C

D

END OF LESSON 103

A **Write your opinion about what Greg should do.**

Greg has saved over $300. He wants to buy a new bike that has racing handlebars, but the bike he has is in good shape. The new bike costs $350 but he could get at least $100 for the bike he has. In your opinion, what should Greg do?

Greg has a problem. ▮▮▮▮▮▮▮▮▮▮. In my opinion, Greg should ▮▮▮▮▮▮▮▮. I think this is a good idea ▮▮▮▮▮▮▮▮. That's why I think Greg should ▮▮▮▮▮▮▮▮.

B

END OF LESSON 104

A **Write a report.**

Something that Was Easy for Me

It was easy for me to learn how to (tell what). It happened (tell when). I was (tell where). (Tell more about what happened.)

B **Find the meaning of each red word in an online dictionary.**

1. They were looking for the home of unicorns and fairies.

2. The fish tank had an oval shape.

INDEPENDENT WORK

C **Put these words in alphabetical order. Word 1 is fire.**

1. ▬▬▬▬
2. ▬▬▬▬
3. ▬▬▬▬
4. ▬▬▬▬
5. ▬▬▬▬
6. ▬▬▬▬
7. ▬▬▬▬

join
garden
lemon
fire
island
hotel
kind

END OF LESSON 105

A Write your opinion about what Ann's family should do.

> Ann's family wanted to go to Wally Park. Wally Park was 300 miles away. Her dad wanted to drive there because he was afraid to fly. Everybody else wanted to fly there. In your opinion, what should the family do?

A Family Problem

- Tell about the problem.
- Tell what you think the family should do.
- Give two reasons.

That's why I think ████████████████ .

B Find the meaning of the red words in an online dictionary.

1. Everybody was on board with my idea.
2. The image was very small.

INDEPENDENT WORK

C Put the words in alphabetical order.

> a b c d e f g h i j k l m n o p q r s t u v w x y z

kitten   officer   argued

dance   lifeboat   half

END OF LESSON 106

A **Write a report.**

How did somebody help you?

How Somebody Helped Me

1. when 3. why 5. how

2. where 4. who 6. after

B **Find the meaning of the red words in an online dictionary.**

1. They saw a large heron in the stream.

2. He ran into her, but he didn't do it on purpose.

INDEPENDENT WORK

C **Put the words in alphabetical order.**

a b c d e f g h i j k l m n o p q r s t u v w x y z

label enormous decide

middle captain forever

END OF LESSON 107

A **Write about your favorite pet.**

My Favorite Pet

- Tell what your favorite pet would be.

- Give reasons why you would like that pet.

I may never have a pet ▆▆▆▆▆▆▆▆▆ , but

▆▆▆▆▆▆▆▆▆▆▆▆▆▆▆▆▆▆▆ .

B **Write the words in alphabetical order.**

a b c d e f g h i j k l m n o p q r s t u v w x y z

1. ▆▆▆▆▆

2. ▆▆▆▆▆

3. ▆▆▆▆▆

4. ▆▆▆▆▆

5. ▆▆▆▆▆

6. ▆▆▆▆▆

blew

boast

billows

beyond

building

breath

C **Find the meaning of the red words in an online dictionary.**

1. I had to drop off some books on my way to the store.

2. She decided to stick around until the game was over.

END OF LESSON 108

A **Find the meaning of the underlined words in your dictionary.**

1. descend

   They will <u>descend</u> the hill.

2. harpoon

   The sailor came home with an old <u>harpoon</u>.

3. lack

   Her house <u>lacks</u> a view.

B **Write a report.**

> What are the three most interesting things you learned in school this year?

The Three Most Interesting Things I Learned

Here are the three most interesting things I learned this year. I learned ▮▮▮▮▮▮▮▮▮▮ . I also learned ▮▮▮▮▮▮▮▮▮ . I also learned ▮▮▮▮▮▮▮▮ .

END OF LESSON 109

A **Write your opinion about a good place to visit.**

A Place I Would Like to Go

- Tell where you would like to go.
- Give two reasons why you would like to go there.

I hope ████████████████████████████ .

B

Life Cycle of a Frog

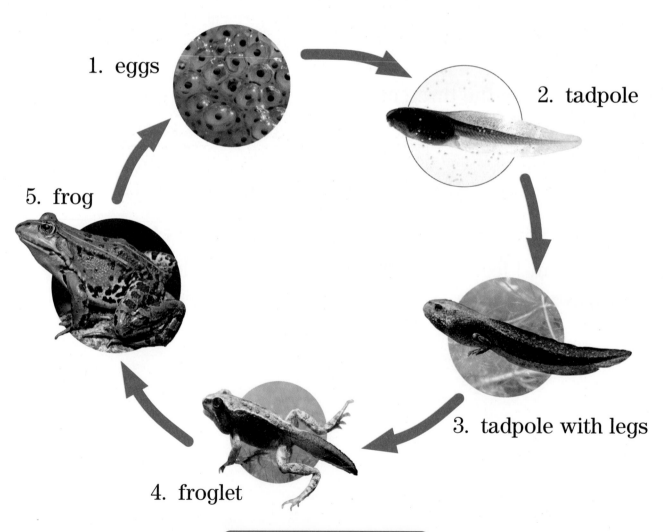

1. eggs

2. tadpole

5. frog

3. tadpole with legs

4. froglet

END OF LESSON 110

A IMPORTANT WORDS

1. koala
2. kangaroo
3. paw
4. eyesight
5. fingerprint
6. Australia
7. eucalyptus

Life Cycle of a Frog

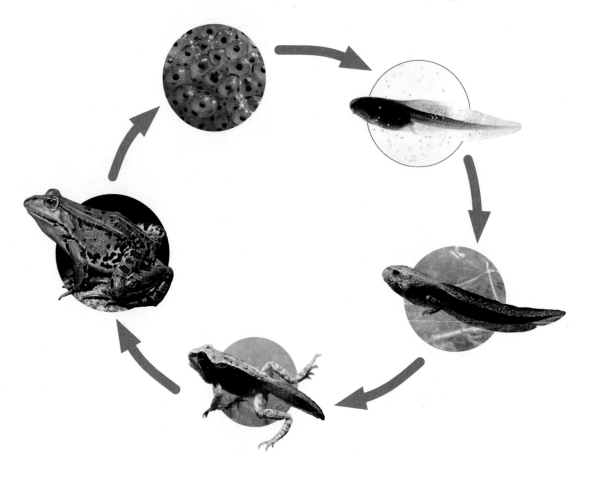

froglet   tadpole

- Write the title.
- Start by telling how many parts the cycle has.
- Name the parts of the cycle.
- Tell what happens in each part.
- Tell why it is a cycle.

END OF LESSON 111

A **Write the correct meaning.**

1. She will <u>deduct</u> the correct amount.

   - take away   • add   • make

2. She collected three <u>morsels</u> of food.

   - bags   • cups   • small pieces

B **Write a report.**

> What is something you are sorry about?

Something I Am Sorry About

I did something that I am sorry about (tell when). I was (tell where).

- What did you do?
- Why were you sorry about it?
- What happened later on?
- How did you feel?

C IMPORTANT WORDS

1. fingerprint
2. Australia
3. koala
4. paw
5. eucalyptus
6. kangaroo
7. eyesight

D KOALA BEARS

Koala bears are not really bears. Koalas are much smaller than bears. Full-grown koalas are the size of a bear cub and only weigh about 30 pounds.

Koalas live in the forests of Australia. They sleep during the day and eat during the night. They sleep 16 to 18 hours each day.

Koala bears eat only one kind of food—leaves of eucalyptus trees. They eat as much as 2 pounds of leaves each night.

Koalas have poor eyesight, but they have a very good sense of smell. They use their sense of smell to find the kinds of eucalyptus they like.

Eucalyptus leaves have water inside them. When koalas eat these leaves, they get enough water, and don't have to drink any other water.

The koala's powerful legs have sharp claws. Each paw has 5 fingers. Some of the fingers work like a thumb. Koalas are one of the few animals that have fingerprints.

Koala Babies

Koalas are in the same family as kangaroos. Female koalas have pouches, like the pouches kangaroos have.

When a baby koala is born, it is less than an inch long. It has no hair. It is deaf and blind. But it crawls into its mother's pouch and lives there for five months. When the baby leaves the pouch, it joins the other koalas and eats with them during the night and sleeps with them during the day. Koalas can live as long as 18 years.

END OF LESSON 112

A IMPORTANT WORDS

1. crocodile
2. pointed
3. dangerous
4. saltwater
5. dinosaur
6. male
7. female
8. hatch
9. Australia
10. Africa

B FACTS ABOUT CROCODILES

Crocodiles are large animals that have sharp teeth and spend most of their time in the water. The maps show parts of the world where crocodiles live. Most crocodiles live in Africa and Australia.

You'll find most crocodiles in lakes and rivers that have fresh water.

There are 23 different kinds of crocodiles. The largest is the saltwater crocodile. It lives near salt water. Some saltwater crocodiles are 18 feet long. That's as long as a large car. Some of these crocodiles weigh more than 2000 pounds.

The smallest crocodiles are less than 5 feet long and weigh no more than 70 pounds.

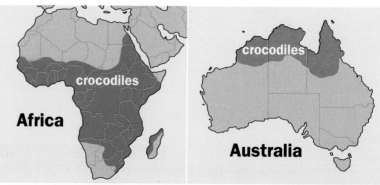

Crocodiles have been on Earth for 240 million years. That means the first crocodiles were on Earth when the first dinosaurs were on Earth.

All crocodiles eat other animals. Here's a picture of a crocodile's mouth. Some of its teeth are large and pointed. Those teeth show you that crocodiles don't chew the things they eat. They rip parts off with their sharp teeth and swallow them in one big gulp.

Female crocodiles lay piles of eggs in a nest. Each pile has 20 to 60 eggs. The female crocodiles take care of the eggs for 3 months.

If the temperature is above 88 degrees during the three months, all the babies will be male. If the temperature is below 88 degrees on some days, most of the babies will be female.

Crocodiles are very difficult to train. They do not have a brain as large as the brains of cats or dogs, so crocodiles can't learn as much as cats and dogs learn.

C Write the correct meaning.

1. She emptied the bucket of <u>cinders</u>.

- small bits of plastic   • clumps of dirt   • partly burned coal

2. The <u>expense</u> for the party was too much.

- noise   • money spent   • people invited

Write a story.

The Anderson Family
Goes Camping

vacation	decided	finally	before
after	weather	poured	soaked

Facts:

- The Andersons went to Lazy Lake.

- Lazy Lake is 80 miles from their home.

- The family has a very large van.

- Their vacation lasted 4 days.

A **Write a report.**

Are Crocodiles Good Pets?

Crocodiles ▮▮▮▮▮▮▮▮ . Crocodiles ▮▮▮▮▮▮▮▮

▮▮▮▮▮▮▮▮▮▮▮▮▮▮ . (Give 3 reasons.)

A better pet would be ▮▮▮▮▮▮▮ . (Tell why.)

B **GOOD STORIES ABOUT THE ANDERSON FAMILY**

- You named some of the people in the family.
- You told where they went on vacation.
- You used words like: **first, then,** and **next.**
- You told how they felt about the rain.
- You wrote a happy ending.

END OF LESSON 115

A **Work in a group to answer the questions.**

1. What is hibernation?

2. What are some animals that hibernate?

3. Why do animals hibernate?

4. How do some animals get ready to hibernate?

5. How long do different animals hibernate?

6. What do animals do when they wake up after hibernating?

• Internet search: hibernation facts for kids

END OF LESSON 116

A **Say a long sentence for each item.**

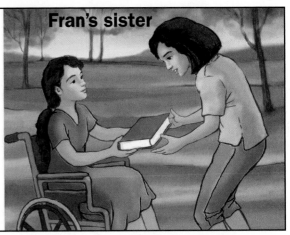

END OF LESSON 117

A Use a dictionary to find the correct spelling.

1. terce   2. berth

   terse   burth

B Say a long sentence about these pictures.

Lily

C Find the meaning of the red words.

1. I wish Al would pipe down.

2. Tonya was the only person who didn't give the plan a thumbs up.

END OF LESSON 118

A Use a dictionary to find the correct spelling.

1. trial
   tryal

2. wod
   wad

3. growch
   grouch

B Say a long sentence for each item.

A Use a dictionary to find the correct spelling. Then write the word.

1. tuch
   touch

2. meal
   meel

B IMPORTANT WORDS

1. desert

2. rainfall

3. temperature

C DESERTS

Deserts are places that are very dry. They get very hot during the day, but very cold at night. Rain does not fall often in a desert, but when rain falls, it may make a flood.

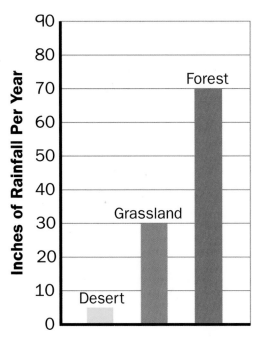

The chart shows how many inches of rain fall each year in different places. These places are deserts, forests, and grasslands.

Deserts get about 5 inches of rain every year. That much rain could fall in one thunderstorm in other places.

There are very few animals in the desert because there isn't water for them to drink. Forests get about 70 inches of rain every year. That is enough water for animals to drink all year round. Also, trees grow well in forests.

A week or two after rain falls in the desert, many flowers bloom. The picture below shows a desert with flowers blooming.

Deserts are very hot during the day but cool at night. Temperatures during the day may be more than 100 degrees. The same place may be around 40 degrees at night.

The temperature drops so much because the air is dry,

even when it rains. Dry air cools much faster than damp air. So when the sun sets in the desert, the temperature drops quickly. That change in temperature is too much for most animals.

D Write a response.

	We spent two weeks walking in the desert,
	and how many animals do you think we saw?
	We saw only one animal. It was a large bird
	that was flying near the edge of the desert.
	I wonder why we didn't see more animals.

- Tell the main reason they didn't see more than one animal.
- Give other reasons.
- Tell where they should go to see more animals.
- Tell why they will see more animals in the other place.

A WORDS WITH MORE THAN ONE MEANING

1. left

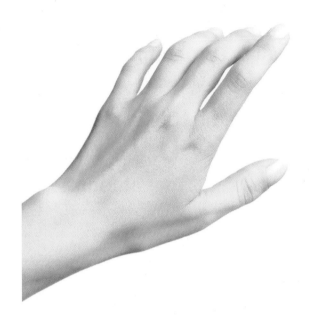 

2. fly

   The fly was on the table.

   The birds always fly over the lake.

3. box

   Her brother was teaching her to box.

   The box was made of cardboard.

4. bark

B THINGS YOU SHOULD KNOW ABOUT WATER

1. the boiling temperature of water

2. the freezing temperature of water

3. the freezing temperature of salt water compared to the freezing temperature of fresh water

4. the weight of fresh water compared to the same amount of salt water

5. the weight of water compared to the same amount of oil

C Work in a group to answer the questions.

1. How do steam engines use water to pull trains?

2. How can water wheels be used to run machines?

3. How do clouds make rain?

4. How do farmers water crops?

INTERNET SEARCHES

- steam engine facts for kids
- water wheel facts for kids
- rain cloud facts for kids
- watering crops facts for kids

END OF LESSON 121

A WORDS WITH MORE THAN ONE MEANING

> 1. bit   2. foot

B **Write the letter of the picture that shows the correct meaning.**

1. The box was more than a <u>foot</u> long.

2. She <u>bit</u> into the bread.

3. A <u>bit</u> of gold was on the shelf.

4. His <u>foot</u> was sore.

A.

B.

C.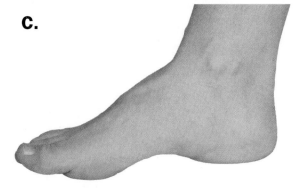

D.

END OF LESSON 122

A WORDS WITH MORE THAN ONE MEANING

1. bat

2. sink

B Write the letter of the picture that shows the correct meaning.

1. The clothes were soaking in the <u>sink</u>.

2. He swung the <u>bat</u> as fast as he could.

3. The boat started to <u>sink</u>.

4. A <u>bat</u> lives in our garage.

A.

B.

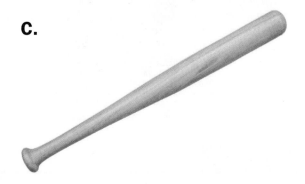

C.

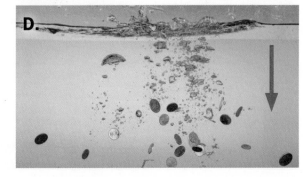

D.

C WAYS OF CUTTING FOOD

DICE

CHOP

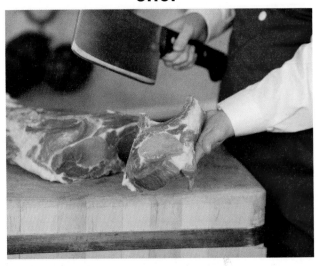

GRIND

SLICE

A WORDS WITH MORE THAN ONE MEANING

1. clip

2. star

B **Write the letter of the picture that shows the correct meaning.**

1. The sky was filled with <u>stars</u>.

2. Tomorrow, she is going to <u>clip</u> my hair.

3. The papers were held together with a large <u>clip</u>.

4. He has been a <u>star</u> for 15 years.

A.

B.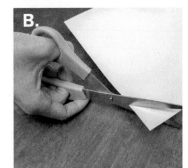

C.

D.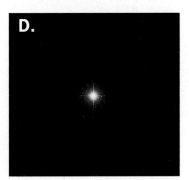

C **Write the words in order from making the biggest pieces to the smallest pieces.**

slice   grind   dice   chop

END OF LESSON 124

A WORDS WITH MORE THAN ONE MEANING

1. seal   2. hard

B Write the letter of the picture that shows the correct meaning.

1. We saw eight <u>seals</u> at the zoo.

2. Make sure you <u>seal</u> the envelope well.

3. The concrete was too <u>hard</u> to break.

4. That test was very <u>hard</u>.

A.

B.

C.

D.

chop   dice   slice   grind

1.

2.

3.

4.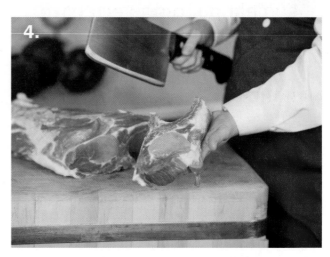

END OF LESSON 125

Glossary

A

adults *Adults* are grown-ups.

adventure When you have an *adventure,* you do something very exciting.

ahead *Ahead* is another word for *in front.*

allow When you *allow* somebody to do something, you permit that person to do it.

although In some sentences, *although* is another word for *but.*

amazing Something that is *amazing* is very hard to believe.

amount The *amount* of something tells how much there is.

ancient Things that are *ancient* are very, very old.

animal preserve An *animal preserve* is a place that protects animals.

ankles Your *ankles* are the joints right above your feet.

announce When you *announce* something, you let others know about it.

apart Things that are not close to each other are far *apart.*

appear When something first comes into sight, it *appears.*

appliances *Appliances* are machines that are used around the house.

approach When you *approach* something, you move toward it.

argue When you *argue* with someone, you tell why you don't agree with what that person says.

argument An *argument* is what you say to make people believe you.

army An *army* is the group of people that goes to war for a country.

arrange When things are *arranged,* the things are in place.

ashamed When you feel *ashamed,* you feel that you've done something bad.

ashes The stuff that is left over after something burns up is called *ashes.*

at bat When a person is *at bat* in a baseball game, that person has a turn at hitting the ball.

attach Something that is *attached* is connected.

attack When people *attack,* they do something to start a fight or a battle.

attention When something catches your *attention,* you know it's there.

Australia *Australia* is the name of a country.

awful Something that is *awful* is very bad.

B

battered When something is *battered,* it is beaten up.

battle A *battle* is one of the smaller fights that take place in war.

behave The way you *behave* is the way you act.

beyond a doubt When you know something *beyond a doubt,* you know it for sure.

billows *Billows* are large clouds or waves that are swelling up.

binoculars *Binoculars* are powerful glasses that make far-off things look close.

blade The *blade* is the flat part of a tool that is connected to a handle.

blame When you say that things went wrong because of somebody else, you *blame* that person.

boast *Boast* is another word for *brag.*

boiled Things that are *boiled* are cooked in bubbling hot water.

booms When a voice *booms,* it's very loud.

bow (rhymes with *how*) The *bow* is the front of a ship.

bow (rhymes with *how*) When you *bow,* you bend forward.

broiled Things that are *broiled* are cooked over an open fire.

buried When something is *buried,* it has things piled on top of it.

C

Canada *Canada* is one of the countries of North America.

captain The *captain* of a ship or plane is the person in charge of the vehicle.

cargo *Cargo* is what ships carry from one place to another.

catch your breath When you *catch your breath,* you breathe very hard.

cave A *cave* is a hole in the ground that is big enough for people or animals to go into.

center The *center* of something is the middle of the thing.

centimeters *Centimeters* are used to tell how long things are. There are 100 centimeters in a meter.

certain *Certain* is another word for *sure.*

championship A *championship* is a contest between the two best teams.

character A *character* is a person or animal in a story.

Chicago *Chicago* is a large city near the middle of the United States.

chilled When you feel cold, you feel *chilled.*

China *China* is a large country near Japan.

claim When you *claim* something, you say it's yours.

clomping A *clomping* sound is the sound a horse makes when it walks on a street.

clue *Clues* are hints.

coach A *coach* is the person who gives orders to the players on a team.

coast The *coast* is where the land meets the ocean.

coconuts *Coconuts* are fruits with heavy shells.

Columbus The name of the man who sailed across the ocean and discovered America is *Columbus.*

completely *Completely* is another word for *totally.*

Concord *Concord* is the name of one of the first towns in the United States.

confusion When things are very strange and mixed up, we say things are thrown into *confusion.*

constantly Things that go on *constantly* go on all the time.

construct When you *construct* something, you *build* it.

consultant A *consultant* is a person who is hired for a special job.

contest Any game or event that has winners and losers is a *contest.*

continue If something *continues,* it keeps on going.

convince When you *convince* people, you make them believe something.

copilot A *copilot* is the person who works with the pilot in flying the plane.

correct *Correct* is another word for *right.*

cottonwood *Cottonwood* trees are large trees.

count on When you can be sure of something, you can *count on* that thing.

couple A *couple* of things is two things.

crate A *crate* is a wooden box that is used to ship things.

creek A *creek* is a small stream.

crouch When you *crouch,* you bend close to the ground.

current *Currents* are places where water is moving.

customer A person who buys things at a store is a *customer* of that store.

 D

damage If you do *damage* to something, you break part of it or ruin it.

danger When you're in a place where you could get hurt, you're in *danger* of getting hurt.

dates *Dates* are small sweet fruits that grow on some palm trees.

deaf People who are *deaf* cannot hear anything.

decision When you make a *decision* to do something, you make up your mind to do it.

defeat *Defeated* is another word for *beaten.*

degrees You measure temperature in *degrees.*

demand When you *demand* an answer, you insist on it.

Denver *Denver* is a large city about halfway between Chicago and San Francisco.

describe When you *describe* something, you tell how it looks or how it works.

destroy If you ruin something so it can't be fixed, you *destroy* that thing.

direct Things that are *direct* are straight and simple.

disappear When something *disappears,* you can't see it anymore.

discover The person who is the first to find something is the person who *discovers* that thing.

distance The farther apart things are, the bigger the *distance* between them.

double *Double* means *two times as much.*

dozen *Dozen* is another word for *twelve.*

drifts When something *drifts,* winds or currents make it move slowly.

dull Things that are boring are *dull.*

during If something happens *during* the night, it happens while the night is going on.

 E

eager When you're *eager* for something, you are really looking forward to it.

earplugs *Earplugs* are rubber things that you put in your ears. It is hard to hear when you are wearing earplugs.

Earth *Earth* is another name for our world.

earth *Earth* is another word for *dirt.*

echo When you hear an *echo,* you hear a sound that is repeated.

effort Something that takes a lot of strength takes a lot of *effort.*

Egypt *Egypt* is the name of a country.

electric Things that are *electric* run on electricity, not on fuel.

electricity *Electricity* is the power you get when you plug things into wall outlets.

encyclopedia An *encyclopedia* is a large set of books that gives information about anything you can name.

engine The *engine* of a vehicle is the part that makes the vehicle run.

England *England* is a country that is almost 4 thousand miles from the United States.

English *English* is the name of the language that people speak in England and the United States.

enormous *Enormous* means *very, very large.*

eohippus *Eohippus* is the first kind of horse that lived on Earth.

equipment Large machines and tools are called *equipment.*

escape When you *escape* from something, you get away from it.

examine When you *examine* something, you look at it closely.

except *Except* is another word for *but* in some sentences.

exit When you *exit* a place, you leave the place.

expensive Things that cost a lot of money are *expensive.*

explain When you *explain* something, you give information about that thing.

expression The *expression* on your face shows what you're feeling.

F

facts Sentences that give you information are *facts.*

fades When something *fades,* it slowly disappears.

fail The opposite of *succeed* is *fail.*

faint When you *faint,* you pass out.

famous If something is *famous,* it is well-known.

fancy If an office is *fancy,* it is not plain.

fear If you *fear* something, you are afraid of it.

field goal A *field goal* is a score in football that is made by kicking the ball.

figure out When you *figure out* something, you learn it.

finally *Finally* means *at last.*

finest Something that is the *finest* is the most expensive or the best.

fired When you are *fired* from a job, you are told you can't work at that job anymore.

flight attendant A *flight attendant* is somebody who works on a plane and takes care of passengers.

force A *force* is a *push.*

forever If something lasts *forever,* it never never ends.

foul *Foul* is another word for *bad.*

frequently *Frequently* is another word for *often.*

frisky *Frisky* means *playful* or *full of energy.*

frost *Frost* is frozen water that forms on grass during cold nights.

fuel *Fuel* is what engines burn when they run.

G

galley The *galley* is the kitchen on a plane or ship.

garden A *garden* is a place where you grow flowers or vegetables.

gift A *gift* is another way of saying a *present.*

globe A small model of Earth is called a *globe.*

glows When something *glows,* it gives off light.

go out for a team When you *go out for a team,* you show the coach how good you are.

grain *Grain* is the seed of grass or cereal plants.

gram A *gram* is a very small unit of weight.

graph A *graph* is a kind of a picture that has lines or parts that show different amounts.

great *Great* is another word for *wonderful.*

Greece *Greece* is the name of a country.

groceries The food that you buy at the supermarket or grocery store is called *groceries.*

grove A *grove* is a small group of trees.

guard A *guard* is a person whose job is to protect something.

H

half If you cut something in *half,* you get two pieces that are the same size. Each piece is half.

harm *Harm* is another word for *hurt.*

hay *Hay* is dried grass that horses and cows eat.

heat When things feel hot, they give off *heat.*

herd A *herd* of animals is a group of animals that run together.

hoist When you *hoist* something, you lift it up.

hollow Something that is *hollow* is not solid.

home run When a baseball player hits a *home run,* the player hits the ball so far that nobody can get it before the player runs around all four bases.

homonym A *homonym* is a word that sounds the same as another word.

honest When you are *honest,* you tell the truth.

hooves *Hooves* are the kind of feet that deer and horses and cows have. *Hoof* tells about one foot. *Hooves* tells about more than one foot.

huddle When people crowd close together, they *huddle.*

human A *human* is a person.

humans *Humans* are people.

 I

illegal Things that are *illegal* are against the law.

imagining *Imagining* is a kind of thinking.

imitate When you *imitate* somebody, you do exactly what that person does.

important If something is *important,* you should pay attention to it.

impression When you have an *impression* about something, you have an idea about that thing.

in fact Here's another way of saying that something is true: *in fact.*

India *India* is a large country on the other side of the world.

insect An *insect* is a bug that has six legs.

insist When you keep telling that you want something, you *insist* on that thing.

interrupt When you *interrupt* somebody, you start talking before the other person finishes.

involved People who take part in a game are *involved* in the game.

Italy *Italy* is a country near Greece.

 J

Japan *Japan* is a country that is 5 thousand miles from the United States.

jewels *Jewels* are valuable stones.

jungle A *jungle* is a forest that is always warm and wet.

 K

Kennedy Airport *Kennedy Airport* is a large airport in New York City.

koala A *koala* is an animal that looks like a teddy bear and lives in Australia.

lad A *lad* is a young man.

Lake Michigan *Lake Michigan* is one of the five Great Lakes.

language A *language* is the words that people in a country use to say things.

lawn *Lawn* is the name for grass that is well-kept and mowed.

lawyer *Lawyers* are people who help us when we have questions about the law.

lean Something that *leans* does not stand straight up and down.

let somebody down When you *let somebody down,* that person thinks you will help and you don't help.

lighter *Lighter* is the opposite of *heavier.*

lookout A *lookout* is a person who looks in all directions to see if trouble is near.

loss When a ball carrier goes the right way in football, he makes a gain. When he gets tackled before he can make a gain, he makes a *loss.*

lowered When something is *lowered,* it is moved down.

machine A *machine* is something that is made to help people do work.

make sense When things don't *make sense* to you, they are not at all clear to you.

make-believe *Make-believe* is another word for *pretend.*

manage When you have to work hard to do something, you *manage* to do it.

mean When you do what you *mean* to do, you do what you plan to do.

measure When you *measure* something, you find out how long, how hot, how heavy, or how tall it is.

mention When you tell just a little bit about something, you *mention* that thing.

Mexico *Mexico* is one of the countries of North America.

microphone A *microphone* is a tool that picks up sounds.

million A *million* is one thousand thousand.

modern *Modern* is the opposite of *old-fashioned.*

moist Things that are *moist* are slightly wet, not dripping wet.

moments A few *moments* is not very many seconds.

motion When you *motion* to another person, you use your hands or body to show the person what to do.

mumble When you *mumble,* you talk to yourself so others can't understand everything you say.

muscle *Muscles* are the meaty parts of your body that make your body move.

myna A *myna* is a bird.

N

neighbors *Neighbors* are people who live near you or sit near you.

New York City *New York City* is the name of one of the largest cities in the world.

normal *Normal* is another word for *usual.*

normally *Normally* is another word for *usually.*

O

object When you argue that something is wrong, you *object* to that thing.

occasional *Occasional* means *once in a while.*

ocean An *ocean* is a very large body of salt water.

Ohio *Ohio* is a state between Chicago and New York.

open field An *open field* is a place with just grass and no trees.

opposite Hot is the *opposite* of cold.

outcome The *outcome* of an event is the way things turn out.

Pacific Ocean The *Pacific Ocean* is the ocean that borders the west coast of the United States.

packed When things are squeezed into a small space, they are *packed.*

palace A king and queen live in a *palace.* A *palace* is a very large and fancy place.

passenger A *passenger* is someone who rides in a vehicle.

peacock A *peacock* is a very large bird with beautiful feathers.

peek When you sneak a quick look at something, you *peek.*

peel Another name for the skin of an orange is the *peel* of an orange.

per *Per* means *each.*

perfect Something that is *perfect* has everything just the way it should be.

perfectly If you do something *perfectly,* you don't make any mistakes.

perhaps *Perhaps* is another word for *maybe.*

permit When you *let* people do something, you *permit* them to do it.

poison If *poison* gets inside your body, it will make your body stop working and it may kill you.

police officers *Police officers* are cops.

poster A *poster* is a large picture that tells about something.

pouch A *pouch* is a small bag that hold things.

pounds *Pounds* are a unit used to measure weight.

practice Things that you *practice* are things that you do again and again.

preserve When you *preserve* something, you save it or protect it.

president The *president* of a country is the person who has the most power to run that country.

probably If something will *probably* happen, you are pretty sure it will happen.

professional A *professional* is someone who gets paid for doing a job, or playing a sport.

project A *project* is a large job.

prop up When you *prop up* something, you support the thing so it will stay in place.

protect When you *protect* something, you make sure that nothing can hurt it.

puzzled Another word for *confused* is *puzzled.*

pyramid A *pyramid* is a type of building found in Egypt.

Q

queen A *queen* is a woman who rules a country.

R

raft A *raft* is a flat boat.

ramp A *ramp* is a walkway that goes uphill.

raw Food that is not cooked is *raw.*

realize When you *realize* something, you suddenly understand it for the first time.

reason When you tell why you do something, you give a *reason* for doing that thing.

receive When somebody gives you something, you *receive* it.

recognize When you *recognize* something that you see or feel, you know what it is.

referee A *referee* is a person who makes decisions about how a game is played.

refund When your money is *refunded,* it is returned.

relatives Your *relatives* are people in your family.

remain *Remain* is another word for *stay.*

reply *Reply* is another word for *answer.*

report When you give a *report,* you give the facts.

required Things that are *required* are needed.

respond When you *respond* to someone, you answer that person.

rich If you have lots and lots of money, you are *rich.*

rip-off A *rip-off* is a bad deal.

rise *Rise* is another word for *moves up.*

rule A *rule* tells you what to do.

ruler A *ruler* is a tool that you use to measure inches or centimeters.

runway A *runway* is like a large road that airplanes use when they take off.

rushing *Rushing* is another word for *moving fast.*

Russia *Russia* is the name of a very large country.

S

salesperson A person who sells things is a *salesperson.*

San Francisco *San Francisco* is a city on the west coast of the United States.

scales The skin of fish is covered with *scales.*

scar A *scar* is a mark left from a bad cut or burn.

screech A *screech* is a high, sharp sound.

seasons Each year has four *seasons:* spring, summer, fall, winter.

sense Another word for a *feeling* is a *sense.*

service People who offer a *service* do a special job.

several *Several* things are more than two things but less than many things.

shabby Something that is *shabby* is not neat and clean.

shallow *Shallow* is the opposite of *deep.*

show up When you go to a place, you *show up* at that place.

skeleton An animal's *skeleton* is all the bones of the animal's body.

slave A *slave* is a person who has very few rights.

slight Something that is *slight* is not very big.

soldiers *Soldiers* are men and women in the army.

soundly *Soundly* means *completely* or *really.*

Spain *Spain* is a country that is near Italy.

sped *Sped* is another word for *went fast.*

spices *Spices* are things that you add to food to give it a special flavor.

spoiled *Spoiled* children cry and act like babies to make people do things for them.

spy A *spy* is a person who gives important information to the enemy.

stale Food that is *stale* is old and not very good to eat.

stands The *stands* in a ball park are the seats where people sit.

stars The best players are called *stars.*

starve When people have no food to eat for a long time, they *starve.*

stern The *stern* is the back of a ship.

still Another word for *silent* or *peaceful* is *still.*

strength Your *strength* is how strong you are.

stretch When things *stretch* out, they are very wide or very long.

striped If something is *striped,* it has stripes.

strut *Strutting* is a kind of show-off walking.

succeed When you *succeed* at something, you do it the way you planned.

sunken ship A *sunken ship* is a ship at the bottom of the ocean.

support When you *support* something, you hold it up or hold it in place.

supposed to *Supposed to* means *should.*

survive When you *survive,* you manage to stay alive.

swirl When something *swirls,* it spins around as it drifts.

swoop Things that *swoop* move in big curves.

tackle When you *tackle* players in football, you bring them down so their knees hit the ground.

tadpoles *Tadpoles* are baby toads or frogs.

takeoff When an airplane first leaves the ground, it's called the *takeoff.*

talent People with *talent* are people with special skills.

tame *Tame* is the opposite of *wild.*

Texas *Texas* is the second-largest state in the United States.

thaw *Thaw* means *melt.*

thought Something that you think about is a *thought.*

ton A *ton* is two thousand pounds.

touchdown When you score a *touchdown* in football, you take the ball across the goal line.

traffic All the vehicles that are driving on a street are the *traffic.*

treasure *Treasures* are things that are worth a lot of money.

triple *Triple* means *three times as much.*

trunk The *trunk* of a tree is the main part that comes out of the ground.

tumbles When something *tumbles,* it turns over and over.

Turkey *Turkey* is a country near Egypt.

tusks The *tusks* of an animal are huge teeth that stick out of the animal's mouth.

twig A *twig* is a tiny branch.

typist *Typists* are people who type things very neatly.

uneasy When you feel nervous, you feel *uneasy.*

unfair If rules are not the same for everybody, the rules are *unfair.*

unpleasant Things that are *unpleasant* are not nice.

usually Things that *usually* happen are things that happen most of the time.

V

valuable Things that are worth a lot of money are *valuable.*

Viking The *Vikings* were people who lived long ago and sailed to many parts of the world.

village A *village* is a small town.

W

wade When you *wade,* you walk in water that is not very deep.

war A *war* is a long fight between two countries.

warn When you *warn* people, you let them know that trouble is near.

warts *Warts* are little bumps that some people have on their body. Toads have warts, too.

water strider A *water strider* is an insect that can walk on the top of water.

weak *Weak* means *not strong.*

weather When you tell about the *weather,* you tell about the temperature, the wind, the clouds, and if it is raining or snowing.

weigh When you measure how many grams or pounds something is, you *weigh* it.

weight The *weight* of an object is how heavy that object is.

well A *well* is a deep hole in the ground.

wise Someone who is *wise* is very smart.

woven Things made of cloth are *woven.*

wrap When you *wrap* a package with paper, you put paper around it.

Y

yard A *yard* tells how long things are. A yard is almost as long as a meter.